All Work, No Play

by Susan Markowitz Meredith

Do you like playing with your friends? Do you have fun in school?

What if you could not play or go to school? What if you had to go to work every day?

A long time ago, many children had to work. They did not have time to play with their friends. They could not go to school.

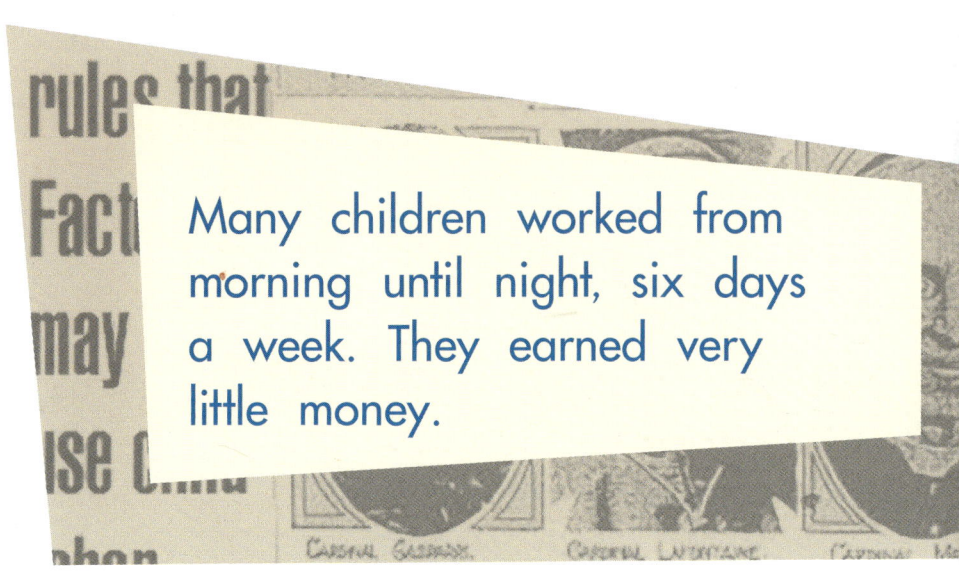

Many children worked from morning until night, six days a week. They earned very little money.

Many children worked in factories. Work was very hard. Many children got sick or hurt doing their jobs.

These children worked in a factory. Factories were big and noisy.

These children worked in a coal mine. The air in the dark mines was thick with coal dust. Many children got sick working in the mines.

Most working children came from families that were poor.

Some working children had to live away from home.

Groups of children stayed in buildings near their workplace.

Many people did not think it was fair for children to have to work. They tried to change things.

Some people marched and made signs to say that children should not have to work.

People wrote stories for magazines and newspapers saying that it was not fair to make children work.

Working children spoke up for themselves, too.

They wanted to play.
They wanted to go to school.
They asked people to help.

After many years, rules were made to help children. Children no longer had to work. They could play and go to school.

Today, most children do not work. But some children still have to. Do you think this is fair? It would be nice if one day all children could play and go to school.